# COUNTERPOINT

# COUNTERPOINT

## Poems by David Alpaugh

STORY LINE PRESS
1994

Published by Story Line Press, Inc.
Three Oaks Farm, Brownsville, OR  97327

This publication was made possible thanks in part to the generous support of the Nicholas Roerich Museum, the Andrew W. Mellon Foundation, and our individual contributors.

Alpaugh, David, 1941-
        Counterpoint / by David Alpaugh.
            p.  cm.
        ISBN 0-934257-55x-8 paper: $11.95

# ACKNOWLEDGMENTS

Some of these poems have appeared or will appear in the following journals and anthologies:

*Asylum Annual,* "Impromptu Meeting In The Falklands", "Herbie"; *Bakunin,* "Wild Card"; *Berkeley Poetry Review,* "Soul Food"; *Blue Unicorn,* "Cleaning The Pool"; *Bogg,* "Counterpoint"; *Exit 13,* "In Praise of Upward Mobility"; *Exquisite Corpse,* "Egbert: One Of The Heroes Of My Memory"; *Feh,* "At The Poetry Reading"; *Footwork, the Paterson Literary Journal,* "On The Raritan, 1959"; *Grasslands Review,* "Unrefined"; *Green Fuse,* "Question Marks", "Psittacosis", "Trail Mix"; *Howling Dog,* "Scaring Vegetarians"; *Hummingbird,* "On Being Asked Where He's Been These Twenty Years", "My Daughter At The Age Of Reason", "The Young", "The Jeweler"; *Piedmont Literary Review,* "Parting My Hair At Fifty-Two"; *Poet & Critic,* "Hunger Artists"; *Poetry Motel,* Part II of "The Earthworm Odyssey" published as "Billy's Way"; *Poetry Flash,* "Many Mansions"; *Poets On:,* "Lament For My Lost Etcetera", "Electronic Epitaph", "Finding The Hen"; *Poultry,* "Late Lunch With Mary Jane"; *Pudding,* "As We Watch MacNeil-Lehrer"; *The Sucarnochee Review,* "The Second Water Poet Reviews His Poems"; *Thema,* "At The World's End"; *The Tomcat,* "Awake!"; *Vol. No.,* "POW"; *Wind,* "Rollfast"; *Wisconsin Review,* "What Happened At 5:15"; *ZYZZYVA,* "After The Perfect Dive."

"A California Ad Man Celebrates His Art" first appeared in the anthology *The Irreversible Man* (Pacificus Foundation, 1991); was reprinted in *The Literature of Work* (University of Phoenix Press, 1991) and *Playground Propaganda* (California State University, Fullerton, 1992). Excerpts also appeared in *AdWeek,* February 1, 1993.

"Hunger Artists" was reprinted in *Rambunctious Review* as a prize winner in their contest for poems on "Hunger."

"The Second Water Poet Reviews His Poems" won *The Sucarnochee Review* Award for Poetry, 1993.

The author is grateful to the following poets who read all or part of this book early on and offered encouragement and advice: Lewis Alpaugh, Richard Callin, Ruth Daigon, Sharon Fain, James Garvey, Lynne Knight, Robert McNally, Richard Silberg, Lisa Sitkin, Hannah Stein, Gerald Stern, John Waldman, Harold Witt—and Zel Latner whose spirit is with me.

FOR MARY JANE

and for my poetry buddy
Janet

# CONTENTS

## III. SOUL FOOD

# COUNTERPOINT

*What lovely echoes, the prisoners said,*
*what a fine musical place to live.*

—Stephen Dunn, *Allegory of the Cave (1990)*

## ON BEING ASKED
## WHERE HE'S BEEN THESE TWENTY YEARS

*Before*
*he springs*
*the leopard lies in the grass*
*watching, listening*
*judging distances*
*making*
*the LEAP*
*in his mind.*

*You always find him looking ahead.*
*You never find him looking behind.*

# I.

## ELECTRONIC EPITAPH

# LAMENT FOR MY LOST ETCETERA

I want to hear spring peepers
the way I did in 1948.
See a thousand shooting stars
without paying five hundred bucks
for a weekend at Ventana.

I want to eat a jujube.
Feel shoebutton paper
on my uneducated palate.
Smoke a licorice pipe.

I want to stand on tiptoe
at the candy counter
in John & Jean's delicatessen.
Drive a couple crazy
with the great debate
that only penny candy can create.

I want to race down to Majesky's —
the first on my block
to buy the latest Captain Marvel
and read it aloud to my flock.

I want to sit on the porch
endlessly rocking

with a stack of baseball cards
now worth thousands
and throw away the all-stars
with the bubble gum
so the trivia merchants
won't defile their holy faces.

I want to read poetry again.
Not the way I read Ignatow now
but the way I read Kerouac then.

I want poetry
to be sluttish
and wild —
a pig turned out of its pen:
French Rimbaud via German Brecht
to an énfant americain.

I want to hang around the high school library
till I meet another hoodlum like François
and watch him swing by his glorious neck
till it feels its arse's weight.

I want to hate.  God, I want to hate!

I want to sit in the garden
with William Blake at Rutgers
and taste the ruddy fruit of deceit.

I want to drink
Hires Root Beer
on the rocks
instead of Courvoisier
neat.

I want to smell cunt
for the very first time
and feel the way St. Joseph felt ...

Chant the magic words
"I'll love you *forever*"
as I unclasp a size 32 belt.

I want to meet my father
home from New York
at the Jersey Central station.
Watch a generation of working dads
drop from the train with elation.

I want to sweat in the attic
with Uncle Walter
and the ping pong ball that never broke —
no matter how hard you hit it.
I want to trade chop for chop,
stroke for stroke.
(It's no longer important that I win.)

I want to warn my uncle
of the long life ahead:

that he'll reach ninety-two
and die in a nursing home bed —
that I will not go to his funeral.

Most of all,
I want to remove things from my mind,
deep-six them in the Raritan River:
my father stumbling to the toilet bowl ...
helping my mother change his diaper ...

Jeff's last telephone call ...
Conley raising gun to temple ...
a little boy coming home from school
to find his mother swinging in the closet.

There are letters that I want unsent.
Tears I want unwept.
Promises I wish to Christ I hadn't kept.

Undo! Undo! Stupid stuff!
I want to begin life's game anew.

There are women I'd like to unscrew.

I want "Son of ..."
not "Return to ..."

I'm finished with Part One.

Bring on Part Two ...

## WHAT HAPPENED AT 5:15

As we walked along the railroad track kicking stones
Paul Herschak showed me what the 5:15
had done to his Indianhead penny:
no feathers … no warrior …
just a copper pancake, smooth and wafer-thin,
three times its minted diameter,
with no date or god left to trust in.

I rubbed the pliant metal between my fingers.
It felt good to get so close to the naked ore;
and thrilling to know you could go to jail
for wreaking such violence on a penny.
It would no longer buy you a candy cigarette
but you could drill a hole and put it on a keychain
with your shark's tooth and rabbit's foot.

Yesterday an iron horse had kicked Paul's
penny off the track and thundered on.
Still, you couldn't always count on luck.
Pennies were awfully small; but we all knew
some of them were jinxed — and could derail
the most powerful locomotive.

At 5:15 the Jersey Central Express
would come around the Netherwood bend

and hurtle past us into the Plainfield station.
Paul grinned: "Do you have a penny?"
I dug a shiny new one out of my pocket — 1949 —
and picked some lint off Abraham Lincoln's beard.

Abe peered into the distance as if he could descry
a mighty engine threatening him and we the people;
could hear citizens scream as the 5:15
plunged over the thirty-foot embankment;
could see maimed survivors hobbling about,
stunned, like Union soldiers at Bull Run.
Suddenly I felt sick to my stomach.
*What if my father were early today?*
*What if Dad were on the 5:15?*

The ties began to vibrate.
The locomotive came around the curve.
The whistle wailed. Paul and I turned and looked back.
Then he dared me and dared me and dared me and dared me

till I knelt and put my penny on the track.

## THE JEWELER

Death-resistant ring of severed light —
each blazing gem still moist
on my five-year-old finger.

Fireflies tonight.

## QUESTION MARKS

When we got off our bikes at the top of the hill
swirls of August butterflies came unto us.
*Polygonia* with silver question marks
landing on our wrists, arms and shoulders.

It happened at the end of childhood
in the evening before chimney-swifts tumble.

And we who had always loved cages —
who had ambushed the painted turtles that spring
wading knee-deep into pond and brook
ripping them off rocks and tree trunks

who only last week had traipsed through woods
bruising arms and legs on bramble bushes
itching to put thumb and finger back of the neck
of every garter snake in Union County

We who dared hunt their royal kinsmen
— *Monarchs, Viceroys, Red Admirals* —
through every yard and field on Mariners Place
bearing down on them with cheesecloth netting
knocking them out of the air with tennis rackets
plucking them off ragweed and Queen Anne's Lace
squeezing their abdomens to help them die

the way the book on Lepidoptera said to do it
thrusting pins through their tender bodies
watching unmoved as the snot-green blood
splattered all over our fingers

We who thought we'd keep their powdered wings
from crumbling into dust
by burying them in cigar-box mausoleums

Stood still staring at our arms in disbelief —
watching these emphatic butterflies land and take off
flitting through the branches of the oak trees
reappearing on the periphery like suppressed dreams
then landing so close to our faces
we could read their living punctuation:
illuminated manuscript on finest tissue
drop caps on ephemeral pages
precious silver questions.

Not one of us tried to catch them.

# EGBERT: ONE OF THE HEROES
# OF MY MEMORY

At thirteen I acquired 28 homing pigeons
all given to me  in an act of desperation
by an old man all too deep in pigeon shit
and I watched for weeks at the back door window
waiting for my "breeders" to perform:

"He's feeding her," I'd yell.
"Come quick! You've gotta see this!"
"He's standing on top of her!"
"He's flapping his wings!"
(A not yet fully-throated crooner
ballading avian love
to a not wholly tuned-in family.)

"Not so loud," my father cried.
"Come and eat your smelts," mother implored.
"He's fucking her," my brother muttered dryly.

In the torrid weeks that followed
I saw more true romance
than most men see in a lifetime
and became intimate

with the art of pigeon love:
the strutting, pulsing, bowing, cooing,
the throbbing of the iridescent crop,
the fanning of the tail like a card deck,
the grand advance and quick rush forward,
the nuances the females lavished on their mates,
responding with just the right preen or peck,
or acceptance of regurgitated seed.

And Whitey took Eight O'clock
And Big Blue took Cousin Sadie
And Achilles had an eye for Four-Leaf-Clover
And by the end of the month it was over.

Except for Egbert, singular male:
Egbert found no sweetheart
showed no pigeon passion
just went about his business eating, shitting
oblivious to the coupling all around him.
Nor did he seem unhealthy, impotent or gay —
just disinclined to do what nature bade
which made John Finn (my pigeon-partner) mad.

For this was serious business,
not some dating game,
with a marketing plan that kicked in
with the laying of an egg

and ended with the swing of a hatchet
and fifty cents from Josephine Mszynski,
the Polish lady who lived down the street.

Who had her own name for them: *Squabs* —
a word that reminded us of Indians
and somehow made the cruel work easier.
*Squabs* they were, not *pigeons*,
like naked nothings wrapped in cellophane
with the other paltry poultry at Food Fair ...
and the axe fell before they'd time
to put on adult feathers
and plead their cases fully fledged.

*SQUABS: 50¢.* If I close my eyes
I can still feel the haft in my hand
and see the steam rising from their severed heads
on snowy January mornings
and I see Egbert pecking in the yard.

Egbert stood funny, walked funny
looked like a priest or intellectual,
never waddled onto the dance floor,
just stayed in his room and read —
and although I would have spared him
until the edge of doom, one morning
(while I was practicing  clarinet)

John Finn took Egbert out into the field
and shot him through the neck with an arrow.

And all I could do was bury Egbert
and curse my pigeon-partner, Finn,
knowing even that was unchristian.

Now, thirty-five years later,
this poem and epitaph,
proof that Egbert homes with me still —
that I can never run his image off my reservation:

*Egbert would not play*
*our stinking game of death.*
*Some say it was faulty genes.*
*I say it was humor and intelligence.*
*Egbert: one of the heroes of my memory.*

# HERBIE

was almost eighteen years old.
He loved to wear the kamikaze aviator's cap
his uncle had brought home from Guadalcanal
with the flap always dangling down under his chin
because somebody wasn't paying attention
or didn't know how to snap the buckle in.

One day Herbie asked if he could ride my
little red tricycle.  I looked up and shook
my head, *"No."* Next thing I knew Herbie
was pedaling my trike up Mariners Place —
and I was sitting in the middle of the sidewalk,
crying for my mom and justice

while Howard and the other boys ran after Herbie,
throwing stones and calling him names —
like sparrows pestering a red-tailed hawk

though our big bird had barely spread his
wings before one of my pedals broke off
under the thrust of his size ten sneaker
and Herbie's Wild Ride was over.

This is my earliest memory:
a Mongoloid in an enemy aviator's cap,
pedaling up the street on a tricycle.

I remember the benign smile on his face
as he turned and looked back to let me know
it was nothing personal — just a matter of pure joy.

You can have my fucking tricycle, Herbie.

# COUNTERPOINT

When I get back to the sixth grade
Ronald Reddicker is waiting for me on the baseball diamond ...

for the runt who imagined it would be different this time ...
that I'd get to use one of my older, more athletic bodies
or street smarts I'd picked up along the way
from *West Side Story* and *A Clockwork Orange* ...

that this time I'd hit the ball over the chain-link fence
or failing that beat the shit out of Ronald Reddicker,
Jefferson School's most terrifying bully.

But, alas, I cannot alter the original cast or script.
I step up to the plate — & swing & swing & swing
and lose the game for my teammates all over again ...
and Ronald Reddicker who takes softball seriously
picks up the bat and hurls it in my direction.
I hear it crack against my shins.
The shame is still far worse than the pain.

Outside Ronald Reddicker is King —
a Golden Gloves Champion
who triumphs over all comers
and rules the playground smirk over fist.

Inside I'm Champ —
will be our eighth grade valedictorian
though like Ronald Reddicker I am from
the wrong side of the Jersey Central tracks.

While our gym teacher keeps his heaviest
hitter's hope alive out on the field of dreams
inside they've given up on Ronald Reddicker.
He's almost fifteen; is still in sixth grade;
has been suspended from school a dozen times.

And *we* know more. Last summer Ronald "fucked"
three high school girls under the boardwalk
at Asbury Park. He's told us their names,
even shown us their pictures. *And you must
always believe Ronald Reddicker.* As we do,
thrilled, when he tells us he's robbed
a gas station and a liquor store *at gunpoint.*

Inside, spitballs and the finger.
Ronald tries to humiliate me every chance he gets;
keeps asking for something called a "blow-job;"
sticks his foot out every time I pass his desk.

Except now I know a little more about Ronald Reddicker.
How, while the dice roll me your average Mom & Dad,
Ronald's rolled snake eyes: a suicidal mother / an alcoholic
father who beats the family black and blue for kicks.

So now I know how hard it is for Ronald Reddicker
to get his "ass" to school each morning.

And how unfair that this deeply wounded boy
must go to war — wound and kill and be killed.
For although no one ever looks for "Reddicker"
on America's Wailing Wall his name appears
there with fifty-eight thousand others.

And me? I'll be excused.
A note from my "shrink"
will reach our draft board just in time
with words Ronald Reddicker would surely
laugh at if he could: *psychologically unfit for combat.*

Today before the bell rings Miss Andersen
strolls down the aisle like a goddess
handing back yesterday's spelling test.
Ronald Reddicker has failed again
and doesn't give a shit. My score? 98%.
I remember the rule about i before e
but forget except after c,
misspelling an easy word, *perceive* —
as if to assure Ronald Reddicker
that no one in this room is perfect.

As Miss Andersen hands back my test
her breasts come so close

they almost touch my face.
I get high on the smell of her *Chanel.*

"Why have you come back?" she whispers.

"To learn counterpoint," I reply.

## AFTER THE PERFECT DIVE

At the bottom of the old stone quarry
Craig sat waiting; struggling with emotions
that threatened to overwhelm him
even when witnessing less spectacular feats
than the one about to take place on the cliff
above — where Lenny, still dripping-wet
after an almost perfect dive,
was preparing to leap from Suicide Ledge
one more time.

But first Lenny's sturdy voice tumbled
to the beach below — as he checked to
make sure his friend was watching.
For Craig had been brought along mainly
to admire Lenny's form, Lenny's daring,
Lenny's grace.

And did. Craig loved the way Lenny
exploded from red shale
as if it were Olympic springboard;
loved the supple arc of his troutlike body;
how, each time Lenny made his turn
and seemed to sail straight towards him,
he flashed that breakfast-of-champions smile —

the one Craig would see again in dreams now
forming like clouds above the cliff. He loved
the way the beads of Lenny's backbone
snapped into place
as he straightened his body
and began his descent
into the old stone quarry's deepest swimming hole.

And in Craig's fantasy it ended there
with a miraculous 10 point O — a whoop
of joy, a clean entry, and down, down,
down, with just a hint of foam as Lenny's
toes went under to let the August sky know
that he wouldn't be coming back up for air
or anything else. Who'd want to
after the perfect dive?

But somebody bobbed back up —
face bloody, arms flailing, crying,
*Help me, Craig! I'm hurt!* Then,
head smashed by a jagged rock
brought in with the late spring runoff,
the championship diver went down again
and stayed down.

And the boy at the bottom of the old stone quarry,
with the great big shoulders and the ruined spine,
raced his wheelchair almost to the water's edge

and would have kept going had the sand not stopped him —
shouting into the quarry what he'd only dared whisper
when he woke at night in a spasm or drenched
in his own urine: *God's a dirty bastard, dirty bastard,*
*dirty bastard …*

And the old stone quarry seconded his cries.

## ROLLFAST

What we did that summer evening
was turn our bicycles upside-down
so the seats were on the ground
and the wheels in the air —
then we twirled the pedal round and round
till our knuckles and fingers were white
and we couldn't make out individual spokes:
just a silver blur and an incremental hum
as the wheel sang the song of its appetite.

What we did next was feed the wheel flowers,
flowers not worth putting in a crystal vase
— Trifolium, Dandelion, Queen Anne's Lace —
flowers that thrived on parental neglect
in the unkempt grass by the utility shed
as if to affirm Britannica on weed:
*any plant growing where it is not wanted.*

Who would be afraid of an idle wheel that spat
out handfuls of ragtag flowers, already half dead?
And the bleeding stalks left a stinging answer
in the summer air: perfume we'd count on ever
after — to keep coming at us stronger than before.

Lynne Saughter went first; she thrust in dandelions;
then Bruce Edwards, a single budding clover:

the only sign we'd get that his own tousled head
would test the metaphor's might just two weeks later
when wheels would screech and metal do its work
a few miles west off Willow Pass Road.

It was starting to get dark on Mount Diablo.
We flipped our bicycles right-side-up
and raced around the cul-de-sac like maniacs,
or Dante's damned, or Milton's falling angels,
getting high on the last drops of Daylight Savings
until parents cried, *Oley, oley, in-free.*
Later we fell asleep thanking Schwinn,
Rollfast and whatever gods may be
for the night, the mountain and the wheel
within a wheel — like love, like magic,
like a spell to help us keep our balance,
and make up for bald tires,
as we cycle to the valley floor.

# AT THE WORLD'S END

*In memory of Rebekah Ross Alpaugh*

Once again I have made it
to this one story building in Florida
and have found my way beyond
the Cuban guard at the front desk
watching a rerun of *Fantasy Island*
and the candy-striper coaxing a wobbly old man
into an aluminum walker
to the little corner room at the world's end
and Aunt Rebekah one more time.

Once again she shows me photographs
of people who were part of my childhood
and people I've heard about but never seen:
How pretty she was in pigtails ...
How proud at her eighth grade graduation ...
How healthy on the day she married Uncle Walter.

And there's a middle to reflect on
here at the world's end (though she doesn't
bring the photos out today). And the beginning
of the end's in a shoebox under her bed —
retirement years, full of oranges & lemons,
uneventful, free of snow.

There are no recent photographs.
No one wants to look at Aunt Rebekah's leg
with the tight shiny skin and pools of purple blood
or dwell too long on or try to image up
the leg already claimed by diabetes.

Or admire the candor with which these legs
chide the legs in the photo on the wall
when she posed on the Boardwalk at Atlantic City.
*These are hers. They are now.*
*Even the missing one is hers, now.*

There is not much to do here at the world's end.
This is a place where it can take all morning
to cut your toenails; where a crossword
can take days to finish
under a magnifying glass.

We sit. We embrace.
We remember Aunt Alice.
We remember the house in New Market
and the farm in Hunterdon County,
now a busy shopping mall
but ...

There's not much to say here at the world's end.
It seems more natural to stare at the walls
or look out the window at the birds.

This is not a good place for words.

## CLEANING THE POOL

A peculiar smell. A dead gopher tumbles
out of the pool-sweep bag onto the grass,
minus fur and features ... latex-white ...
no, more the color of a boiled sausage.
For a moment I'm in high school in biology
class, staring at a human fetus in a mason jar.
It's snowing outside. *New Jersey. 1959.* Then I'm
back in this Contra Costa heat, cleaning the pool.
I get a stick and poke the thing around a bit
till what was once a mouth opens and the curved teeth
protrude, quotation marks uneffaced by algaecide,
singing beyond sea-change of what it did /slash/was —
and I'm sure it's a gopher and can spear it with my stick
and hurl it over the fence toward the freeway.

# ELECTRONIC EPITAPH

Hi! Sorry I can't pick up the phone now.
I'm dead.

If you are shocked and want more details
on my struggle with the avenging angel —
press 1 now.

If we have had sexual contact
in the past ten years and you want to be sure
that I really died of cancer —
I'd press 2. If I were you.

For pithy deathbed sayings,
including a stunning rendition of my death rattle
rising nobly over a Windham Hill soundtrack,
press 3. Wheeeeeeeeeeeeeeeeeeeeeeeeeeeeeeeee!

For details on my upcoming cremation
and burial in a Campbell soup can
stay on the line and a mortician will assist you.

You who are calling to collect old debts
or initiate new friendships, what can I say?
I'm dead.

Or if you're that telemarketer
who keeps leaving cheerful messages
regarding what you call my "portfolio" —
maggots are up ten points, pal,
I'm dead.

Most alluring of my long-lost college sweethearts
I knew you'd phone me by and by
to say hi and whisper directions to your bed.
I'm sure you're still a knockout.
Sorry I missed your call.
No, I can't join you for a drink tonight,
I'm dead.

Teacher who assured me my poetry was nought
and urged me to write a book on *Piers The Plowman,*
the "C" version, that is, though "B" needed me too,
as did "A." Lauda, Laudē,
I'm dead.

Like Dante, dead; like Villon, Rabelais, dead;
like Chaucer, Shakespeare, Joe G. Schmo,
and poor Wally Stevens, the insurance man
and Emperor of Ice Cream, dead.

For a brief biography, press 4 ...
to hear me read my poems, press 5 ...
to find out what the eternal silence is like, press 6 ...

7 ... 8 ... 9 ...

for the images they said would flash before my mind
in the final moments, they were right, they did ...
though *why one's history should be burnt into the brain*
*even as memory fails* is an intriguing parting question.

And you whom I have injured ...
you who are impatient to join me ...
you who like hapless Stevie Wonders
have called too late to say "I love you"
and wish you could return to the original menu

please press the star sign, now.

# II.

## TERRESTRIAL LAUGHTER

# THE EARTHWORM ODYSSEY

*As for your earth or angle worm, there are three ways to take*
*Sir Slime prisoner — each governed by a primordial element.*
— Izaak Walton, *The Compleat Angler*


## 1. EARTH

Ach! Heinrich! Grab that spade or trowel!
Revolution's the surest way to free Sir Slime
from the downtrodden topsoils of the earth.
And simplest weapons — shovel, rake, hoe —
are all we need to overthrow the humus ...
release the teeming regolith... liberate the loam ...
until the hero of our uprising —*L. terrestris* —
writhes in grungy glory at our feet.
If you don't mind soiling your hands in his drool
you can pluck him from the dirt with thumb & finger;
or shiver the giant clods into dust through a sieve
till a hundred worms dance naked on the wire.
Erda! Fafnir! This is the way of the people!
Dig deep! and cast your bait into the stream!


## 2. AIR

Stick your pitchfork into the ground
and give it a good shove with your foot,

driving the prongs deep into the soil;
then rock the pitchfork back and forth
applying rhythmic pressure to the haft.
*"Worms are like us,"* Billy Sessler would say,
*"Worms have to breathe — just like us."*
And he forced stale air I didn't even know
was there to fart its way to the surface,
transforming loose dirt into tight, thick clay,
until every worm in the neighborhood
was having an asthma attack, and pretty soon
they were poking their heads out of windows.
*"Here comes everybody!"* Billy Sessler laughed,
as a dozen big ones wriggled into sunlight.
*"I told you they have to breathe — just like us!"*
And I looked at the older boy in awe,
certain I had found my mentor —
because I knew he had not learned this in a book.


### 3. WATER


Three requires a thunderstorm tempestuous enough
to make "nightcrawlers" so fear death by drowning
that they haul their hermaphroditic bodies partway
onto the grass and lie there exposing themselves.
My father would get me out of bed at two AM —
I'd put on galoshes and follow him outside
and we'd sneak across the spongy lawns

armed only with Eveready flashlights.
No sooner would one of those ruddy creatures
darken my beam than I'd drop to my knees
and seize its bulbous head between my fingers
before it could shrink back into the vaginal earth;
then I'd exercise the lanky art of easing a nightcrawler
out of its hole, whole. I was always surprised when it
finally let go, like an exhausted rubber band or spent
penis. I'd deposit my conquest in the can and move on
until every lawn and garden on our street was picked
clean and the knees of my dungarees were sopping
wet and my coffee can full and reeking with their
lather — that startling, earthy, lubricious smell:
*essence of midsummer worm slime.*


## 4. FIRE

"There's a fourth way!" writes Mrs. Jessica Jones
of Toms River, New Jersey:*"You can buy them!*
Haven't you seen those signs along the road
in what our government likes to call 'the rural areas'?
Worm farming *mon petit poète maudit*
is one of this nation's thriving cottage industries.
Thank God we still do *something* better than Japan
because, between you and me,
I'd sooner touch my husband's dickie
than a slimy, suppurating, diggory-delvet earthworm!

May they always be kept in somebody else's cellar;
and if we *must* condescend to fellowship
let glove or tweezer or silk-lined casket
mitigate *the horror!*"


5. ENVOI

Always *three* ways ...
Always a can of worms ...
Always this damp desire to go fishing ....

# ON THE RARITAN, 1959

On the first Saturday in April trout season began.
Half of northern New Jersey converged on the Raritan.
We stood in hip boots, shivering, in cold, muddy water,
some casting flies, others worms or hellgrammites,
trying not to snag the line of that fellow sportsman
who stood just a few dozen feet downstream.
One morning we heard cheering on the other side of the trestle.
Workers from the state fishery at Hackettstown
were stocking the north branch of the Raritan —
flinging shimmering jumbo trout at jubilant fishermen:
hatchery-fed rainbows, so starved for insects and worms,
they began striking the moment they hit the water.
We too cheered when the hatchery barge came into view
*and then some really fine trout fishing began.*
In less than an hour everyone took the legal limit.
I wrapped six keepers in the *Newark Star Ledger*
then joined the convoy heading east on Route 22.
This, I said to myself, is the only way to fish for trout
in New Jersey. That was before I had my first marketing
class and began to question channels of distribution:
Why for instance did the state waste everyone's time
throwing the people's trout into the water
when it would have been more elegant
to drop them right into our creels,
eliminating the middleman,
the river.

## A CALIFORNIA AD MAN
## CELEBRATES HIS ART

For those of you
who come here
out of spite
expecting to hear
a con man apologize —
prepare to gnash your teeth.

I am here to celebrate
the TV commercial —
the authentic poetry of our time:
lovingly produced,
widely received,
technically dazzling —
*It really changes lives.*

My title? "Tubular Poetics."

We deal in time and space:
thirty seconds of sound and light
rolling from earth to sky,
sky to earth,
kitchen to bedroom.

Our spirit is democratic.
We have made a pact
with Walt Whitman
to celebrate fecund America,
embracing all creeds, all colors:
men and women, young and old,
the runt as well as the athlete.

We praise hearth and home
in a manner that Beowulf
would understand.
Our art is tribal, mnemonic...
designed to be sung into the heart
by families gathered round the fire —
not warehoused in a public library
or read in private on a printed page.

Our words are deeds.
Like iron weapons
warriors carry into battle
to brandish at the foe
they must contribute to the victory.
If they don't sell cars or condoms
Grendel comes out of the fen
people lose food, status, power —
and like a singer of unwanted songs
under the castle wall

we are not allowed to get on the elevator
and rise to the thirty-eighth floor.

Like Bert Brecht, we believe that art
is an instrument for social progress.
We are concerned about the sick,
the homeless, those denied justice.
Much of our best work is in praise
of cold tablets, real estate chains,
and motorcycle lawyers —
and every afternoon when school lets out
we suffer the little children to come unto us.

Like all great craftsmen
we find the material reality imposes
only partly to our purpose.
Our task is to build a world elsewhere,
with porcelain teeth, perfect complexions,
fully rounded bosoms and bottoms:
a pastoral living room ...
an electronic bower of bliss ....

Into this world creep many dragons:
zits, dandruff, athlete's foot,
bras that sag or ride up,
bad breath, fatal to love —
relentless fiends called
"Ring Around the Collar,"

"Hemorrhoidal Tissue,"
and surly appliances
that snap, snarl
and refuse to work.

In the cataclysms that ensue
we let good have its way with evil,
demonstrating the wisdom
shown a hundred times each day
by our hero with a thousand faces,
*The Consumer.*

Finally, like Milton
we have the highest moral purpose,
calling upon our Muse to justify
the ways of any product our agency assigns
to whatever target market is specified.

In doing so we've stumbled on free will
and with it a whole new tragic vision:
the knowledge that despite triumphal odes,
hymns, eclogues, paeans, songs of love,
and Juvenalian satire at its bitterest —
millions ignore the good and choose Brand X
dropping down to darkness and perdition.

These are just a few of the qualities
that link us to *The Great Tradition.*

## MANY MANSIONS

On my way home from work this evening, pigeons,
nesting on top of an exit sign on 680 —
creatures that could fly halfway to paradise *fast*,
Point Reyes, Big Basin, High Sierra,
choosing to live amid the noise and miasma
of a relentless California freeway ...
risking carcinogens & drive-by shootings
twenty-four hours a day.

And when I off-ramp into Pleasant Hill, sparrows,
raising a dysfunctional family
in the amber circlet of a traffic light
just a block away from BART.

And me and my wife and our children —
a little further down the line.

## MY DAUGHTER
## AT THE AGE OF REASON

"Will you please get that cat out of your bed!"
I shout, opening Janet's door to say goodbye —
on my way down the hall, out to the garage,
onto the freeway towards work.

"He's full of fleas!"

She draws Marshmallow closer
strokes his white belly
kisses his ears, eyes, nose and whiskers.

"He's full of love," she smiles.

# AS WE WATCH MACNEIL-LEHRER

Janet, our nine year old daughter,
who voted for George Bush
in her fourth-grade mock-election,
expresses her dissatisfaction
with Clinton's first executive order,
restoring public funding for abortion.

"It's stupid," she declares.
"If people would just wear condoms
they wouldn't have to have abortions.
It's not fair to kill babies."

While Gergen & Shields probe the issue,
we do some probing of our own
but discover only the sketchiest
conception of what a condom is
and how, where and by whom
the magic garment is "worn."
Her mother and I fill-in-the-dots
and try to draw a distinction
between infants and fetuses.

We do not tell her that Stephanie,
the teenage babysitter she adores —
who has access not only to condoms

but to jelly, foam and something called
"the pill" — had an abortion last summer
and is scared she may be pregnant again.

On technically firmer ground now,
knowing that a condom
is something like a balloon
that a man puts over his penis
to keep something called sperm
from reaching something called
an ovum, she hardens her position:
*"All men should be forced to wear them."*

My wife and I glance at each other,
remembering our own neglect,
ten years ago, by the fire —
and all that it has brought us.

# IN PRAISE OF UPWARD MOBILITY

We  had ducks in our pool this morning.

Mallards, a drake and his hen. They came
skittering in to what must have seemed to them
a strange body of water and swam around
quacking their approval; tried like good sports
to acquire a taste for chlorine and algaecide;
then hopped ashore and waddled about the patio,
searching for slugs and asking savvy questions:
*A good place to shit? To lay eggs?*

Just another upwardly mobile couple —
checking out real estate on a warm spring day;
looking for a safe, drug-free environment,
a family neighborhood with good schools
and not too many snapping turtles,
where they just might have *that one chance in hell*
to bring up their children in the old duck way.

They flew onto the deck to sun themselves
and were impressed by our view of Mount Diablo.
Nice couple, though their can-we-really-afford-it-dear
giggles made them sound a little sillier than they were.
Feeling at home they ambled back to the pool
where they dove right in and frolicked like honeymooners.

I've always been a sucker for reason. So my
impulse was to wise Candide & Cunegonde up —
to open the window and shout: *"Don't buy here!*
*The schools are full of drugs! All people care about*
*are golf, pizza, television!"*

But knowing how badly a pair of nesting
mallards can foul a swimming pool
I ran outside banging a cookie sheet.

At first they stared at me in disbelief —
much as my wife and I stared at the man at the mall
who appeared out of nowhere shouting obscenities.
But when they saw how I meant to be O! O! O!
so much ruder than your average asshole —
being upwardly mobile, they rose into the air
and, casting one last longing lingering look behind
at a dream they had almost bought into,
beat their way back to their one-bedroom apartment:
26-D, at the duck pond, next to Lucky's supermarket.

## PSITTACOSIS

The danger in cleaning the bird cage
is that you will go to the garage
to get some newspaper
to line the tin tray at the bottom
so your cockatiel can shit on the president's face
or scratch the latest rock-n-roll idol's eyes out
and find yourself mired in yesterday's *Times* —
victimized by stories you neglected to read
or only now half remember:
that Giants game you missed while you were in LA,
an outbreak of Psittacosis in Ohio,
the murder that took place while you were sick with flu
or busy under the covers making early morning love
and you sit there amid the garden tools
and black widow spiders
knocked out by every passing day,
unable to rise up and break away —
to get a feel for today's peculiar weather
or the screaming of a cockatiel

# WILD CARD

At five-fifteen
on a Friday afternoon
preceding the 4th of July
from his hideout
under the bleachers
at the football stadium
or in a subway tunnel
underneath the city
(or a zillion & 1
even zanier retreats —
above, beneath,
beyond the scope
of Interpol
to discover)
after champagne
with his gang of admirers
and fulsome tribute
to his evil genius
THE JOKER
will *cackle*
and flick a switch —
and every traffic light
in America

will turn green
at precisely the same moment.

*I'm Batman.*

This is the kind of shit
I have to put up with every day.

## AT THE POETRY READING

"Kicked out of bed by whores,
clutching my trousers to my groin,
I stumble down the brothel steps
onto the condom littered lawn ..."

"MET–UH–FOR–ICK–LY," *I hope!"*
A matron in the first row interjects.

"Of course, metaphorically,   I stammer.
"Images, similes, tropes ....
How would Hamlet put it?
*Poetry in jest!"*
Then having shown my good breeding
I go on with my reading,
extending my "metaphor"
with zest.

## AWAKE!

There is no need
to open the door
on a Saturday morning
for Jehovah's Witnesses.

One can simply leave them shivering in the rain
and rudely continue to play the clarinet,
reread *Huck Finn* or leap about the room
to the liberating strains of *Mahagonny*.

Show me the law that says we *must* invite them in;
put aside our mirth to attend to their mechanick testimony
or raise their false hopes high pretending to believe in Noah's
Ark — only to ram it good with Darwin's theory.

It is not by accident that my front door has a peephole
worthy of Double-O-Seven. It was installed by Lenny
Bruce to keep the Avon lady from being raped
and the Fuller brush man from winding up
with his company's stiffest product you know where.

They knock. I peek. The lens refracts.
They become rare objects in its prism.
I analyze them like a scientist: curious facts.
Creatures trapped in amber will not hurt me.

They poke their umbrellas in my doormat.
Their rods and their staves they mesmerize me.
They might be tending sheep by Siloa's brook
or chatting with the Lord on Sion's hill.
Or teaching sweet Susannah to sit still.

Were I to open the door I'd find less cause for amusement —
faced with dangerous markings, aggressive tactics
from *A Field Guide to the Religious Fanatics.*[1]

---

[1]*Note well the patronizing smile; garments fiercely
out of style; and an intimidating migratory habit —
traveling in threes; as Holy Trinities; never as mere
man, woman or child.*

---

As prophesied, they arrive bearing gifts —
their arms full of sacred publications.
Like Moses, dismounting from the Mount,
distributing God's Word like kennel rations.

I want to read *Martin Chuzzlewit,*
*The Cantos* of Ezra Pound,
*Finnegan's Wake,* Byron's *Beppo,*
the back (and side) of a Rice Krispies box —
anything but their melancholy Gospels
and partisan religious pamphlets.

"Awake! Awake!" they cry,
gently beating my door down.

(A good missionary can almost *smell* the damned.)
But I am still hung partly over
on last night's Campari and soda:
My heart reaches for the doorknob —
but not my hand.

I watch as they turn and go back down the walk
into the yard of my Unitarian neighbor.
*Clammy skins. Jurassic minds.*
They are laboring under a spell.
I cannot stand their smell.
I will not have them drinking from my goblet.

So, why, now these witnesses flee from me at last,
instead of feeling relief, even exultation,
do I find myself feeling like D. H. Lawrence?
— *ashamed at having thrown a stick at a snake.*
There's a blizzard of excuses I could make—
but when truth catches cold it coughs and sneezes.
I have shut my door to baby Jesus.
The little lambs have come to lie down with the lion
and the lion has driven them away.

They'll be back next Saturday.

# IMPROMPTU MEETING
# IN THE FALKLANDS

*O Columbo, Columbo, a little less art:*
*We know you can see to the bottom of the heart.*


I knew it was going to be a bad day
when I came down for breakfast
and found Lieutenant Columbo in my living room.
His feet were propped up on my coffee table
and the smell of his cigar was everywhere.

He was thumbing through my copy of Rilke
in the Stephen Mitchell translation.
"This Maria's a terrific lady, Sir," he said.
"Real classy. She reminds me of the Missus."

I asked if there had been a murder.
"Oh no, Sir, not a murder," he said.
"I didn't say *murder*, Sir, definitely not
although a number of people are dead.
Just old age, Sir, quietly, in bed."

I asked if he had come about the turtles
the ones I put in a porcelain pan
thirty-eight years ago and left by the furnace
till their odor crept up the cellar stair
and nearly gave my poor mother heart failure.

*"Turtles?"* he asked, letting his bad eye go blank.
"Ah, you've been reading Lowell, Sir," he said.
He rubbed his skull. "Turtles are *nothings.*
You can do what you want with them. Go
ahead. Torture them. Paint their shells red."

I asked if he knew what happened in the sanitarium
when the madwoman came stark naked to my bed:
How I pulled her to me and felt her crazy breasts
until the attendant came and led her back to bedlam.
How she shuddered and rolled her eyes in bliss
proud of her defiant nakedness.

"Columbo! I was only sixteen!" I cried.
"Columbo! I was lost in a dream!" I sighed.
"My nerves were a-jangle with insulin shock
and not knowing what to do with my adolescent cock.
Columbo! I'm innocent!" I lied.

"I know you've been under a strain, Sir.
It's the poetry, and staying up too late.
It's this Rilkee woman, with her Angels, Death & Fate.
It's this Yeets fellow." He winced. *"It's Walter Pater.
Don't be like Liddy, Sir. Avoid that 'gemlike flame.'
I'll let you rest a while and come back later."

I knew if I did nothing he'd turn at the door
and nail me with one of his shitty questions.
So I cried like Faust as he stumbled down the hall,

"Lieutenant Columbo! Don't go! I confess!
Come back. I'll burn my books! Let's play chess!"

"I'm just a detective," he said, eyeing Steppenwolf
"and don't know much about this *Herman Hessee*.
What I do know pretty well is baseball, Sir.
And do you know what's bothering me? These poets
who left the stadium before the game was over:
Sylvia Plath. John Berryman. Anne Sexton.
You're familiar with their work?
Now why would they do that, Sir?
Do you see my point? *It's messy*."

"Maybe they were bored with the game!" I cried.
"Maybe they were tired of watching pitchers spit
of scoreless innings ... of raw drizzly weather ...
of fans egging on players stranded at third:
'Steal home now — and get a head start on forever.'"

"That explains it, Sir!" he said, hitting himself on the
head: "Boredom! Or what do the French say? *Ennui?*
For who would suffer through a pointless game
if he could leave his sorrow in Candlestick Park
get a jump on traffic and be home before dark?"

"But something's bothering me ..."
(he was rummaging in his coat):
"Can you tell me, Sir, how you explain *these?*"
Hard evidence at last. He shoved it in my face.

Three tickets to the World Series.

*"The World Series, Sir!* The hottest seat in town
and climax of the whole damned season!
I'm trying hard to buy this boredom theory,
Sir, but the Missus says it's a pee-pee poor reason."

"Columbo," I said, "I'm going to level with you now
— and fuck you, if you don't believe me —
*The Giant's were losing, losing real bad
and every time they had a chance to turn it around
Dave Dravecky stepped onto the mound to pitch
and his arm fell off."*

"Now get the hell out of here, you Dumbo."

The Lieutenant's cigar exploded
with an elegant fart-like sound
I watched him choke and cough
fight for breath, twirl around,
then suddenly: *no more Columbo.*

I sat there trembling, half-hoping he'd be back
wondering what the hell he was really after.
I turned on TV but the picture stayed black
and I heard terrestrial laughter.

# III.

## SOUL FOOD

# THE YOUNG

are begging theory
to spare them from experience
politics from history
poetics from the line.

Some sprint, some hobble
to the table — all in time
break bread here
gulp the dead-black wine.

# HUNGER ARTISTS

When I stopped eating my food
because it was something I hated
(fried smelts or spam or last week's stew)
or because I'd had a vision
most kids have at five or six
when they stare at their forks and see
not meat *but the flesh of a lamb, a pig, a chicken*
my father would give me a good reason
to finish every morsel on my plate:
*because of the poor starving children in Europe*
who had no food, who were lucky to get
stale bread and a cup of dirty water.
What would they not give to sit at our table
and eat fried smelts off melmac plates?

I learned that fish was brain food;
that milk would strengthen your bones
carrots make you see like a leopard in the dark
but beer, ah, *beer* would put hair on your chest
something I couldn't see much use for at the time.
It was 1948. It was still a sin to waste food.
And having watched Grandma wrapping Christmas
presents — flour and sugar and dried beans —
for our relatives "in the old country"
the guilt hit home. I licked my platter clean.

Years later I found my own way to encourage
my kids to eat. I transformed their plates
into theaters of the absurd — where peas, carrots,
hamburgers could strut their hour upon the stage
disguised as parents, children, household pets.
When one of my daughters dropped a fork and refused
to eat — I'd raise the curtain and whet her appetite:
"Janet! See that stringbean? It's little Tom Dacre.
You've already eaten his mom and baby brother.
Today's Tom's birthday. His friends are waiting
*in your stomach* — to sing and open presents
and eat cake." Janet's eyes would grow large.
She'd raise her fork, stab Tom's slender body,
tenderly, pop him into her mouth, and smile. Fish,
fruit, vegetables got starring or supporting roles
as needed to achieve a balanced diet.
Down in Janet's stomach the mood was festive
as Grandpa Joe, Aunt Lil or Cousin Spike
came splashing down her gullet to join their relatives
as if they were riding the Manteca Waterslide.

Still later when Dad lay dying I sat by his hospital
bed and tried to get him to eat the hospital fare;
and when that didn't work, I hid Mom's pot roast
under my coat and snuck it past Reception
to his room. It never occurred to me to tell him
about the poor starving children in Europe
or the nuclear family singing Happy Birthday
in his gut, waiting for their cat to reappear.

He had had it with chewing and swallowing;
with taking six different kinds of pill; with
spills that got him into trouble with the nurses.
I tried to be a hunger artist; to whet Dad's appetite;
to coax the mischief back into his eyes.
I told jokes. I sang songs. I played the clarinet.
I raised his fork to his mouth again and again
till there I was standing not by my father's bed
but by a highchair watching a grown child cry.
Strained beets. Glucose. The intravenous truth.
*Eat your food, kid. Or you'll die.*

# LATE LUNCH WITH MARY JANE

When I die, I tell my wife,
Burn my body in the fireplace:
You may need a Duraflame log or two
to get me started till I flare up and crackle!
If it's winter, I hope you'll relax in our ratty nauga-
hyde armchair and sip some *Muscat Alexandria*
a dessert wine we once drank after making love
— *light and fruity* but *never cloying* —
while you enjoy the warmth of my body one more time;
then gather up my ashes with your Modigliani smile
and put them in a Campbell's soup can
where I promise to be *mmmm ... mmmm ... good.*
I'd feel awfully stylized in one of those plastic Andy
Warhol's (it seems to me *forever* deserves the real thing).
Not that I wouldn't get a kick out of something gourmet
on the label: Cream-of-a-Sparrow's-Ass or Consommé —
but we both know our croutons ... how they crumble.
So if Safeway only has the Manhandler varieties in stock
or you have a chance to use one of those free coupons
(the ones the baggers give you at the checkout with a wink)
hey, babe, you know I'm with you every day
and something plain like Bean with Bacon's fine.
All I ask is that you think twice before dumping old man Campbell

just because Heinz and Progresso rise up with sexier ads.
But you know how I feel about brand loyalty.
Remember how I kept on loving Frost? Eliot? You?
Long after the Black Mountain Boys had triumphed?

## THE SECOND WATER-POET
## REVIEWS HIS POEMS

*In the early 1600's John Taylor, a man of low birth who made
his living ferrying gentlemen back and forth across the Thames,
published over fifty books of verse and was lionized as "the
Water-Poet" by Ben Jonson and the London literati. By the
time Taylor died in 1653 his poetry was already forgotten. The
fragment that follows is the only surviving work of a "Second
Water-Poet," known only as "Tom," who wrote during the
reign of Charles II, thirty years after Taylor's death.*

All in all, not a bad catch.
I like the way they lie in the creel.
I like the manly contrasts —
Perch on carp on eel on mullet —
Some pastoral and some slobberdegullet.
I like the way the sun shines on their scales,
Colors of a rainbow you only see in pails.

My betters encouraged me, with a curse:
"You've a quick wit, Tom — you ought to try verse."
"It's a lot like rowing — proper use of the oars,
Up and down, smartly now — look at those whores
In the blue boat yonder ...."
                              "Read Suckling, Tom.
He's a great one to cut stylistic eyeteeth on;
And when you've a book, I'll show it to the Earl ...."

"What the world needs now's another water poet,
Tom — *like Charles needs another girl!"*

They need to know that we are living too —
Laughing, sorrowing, enjoying a wench or brew
Breaking our backs to row them 'cross the river
And when the pie's sliced, settling for a sliver.
They need to know that we find them as funny
As they find us; that when they give us money
Only our hands touch; that we want it that way.
They despise our work; we abhor their play.

I wrote these poems for myself. And for Kate.
And Bill. They're full of the streets and river,
Of this daily bread life that's mine, and theirs.
But when I tried to recite them they gave me
Such blank stares, as if I were speaking in tongue!
And Kate started crossing herself and saying her prayers,
And Bill wanted to know how I could give myself such airs,
Reminding me that I was *Tom the Waterman* —
And *Tom the Waterman* would always be.

So there they lay in the still unopened creel
— Fish, poems, images, emotions —
Thrashing so, I'd a mind to throw them back —
Till I remembered: trolling inside the weir at dusk,
As the pike broke water, scrabbling after gnats and flies,
How exciting it was to engage some old Leviathan …
To feel that primal presence commandeer my line.
How hard I fought to coax him to the surface …

How thrilling to see that shimmering form
Come within reach of my net …
How confounded I was when he shook the hook,
Disappearing in a swirl of blood and foam.

Besides, I'd been dared; and longed to be a fisher
Of men; so I wrapped them carefully in paper
And gave them to the ugly hawk-nosed man
Who crosses to his mistress every Thursday
Even as her husband crosses to th'Exchange
(When our wakes cross they salute each other)
And he gave them to this Dryden chap
Who brought them to the pub where Moll serves suds
And Moll told me how they stamped their feet
And struck the board and laughed and jeered
Treating my words like jokes and shouting:
*"Hail to the Water-Poet! Glorious woodnotes wild!"*

Till Dryden told them to shut up and listen —
That if they'd listen honestly they'd catch
Something they none of them could reach,
Not if they wrote a thousand years:
And he read my poems with respect and feeling
While they sulked and smirked into their beers.

I dreamt he came and talked to me, John Dryden
(God knows, I long for healthy talk!)
But nothing — except this simp'ring printer
Who returns my papers like a fishmonger
And begs to show my "genius" to the world.

And if I let them kick my soul about the City
I can make ten pounds and be a "celebrity"
For a while — like that fool before me: *Taylor*.

But a printer can't make me.
Nor a gentleman. Nor God.
*They're mine.* And I've a bolder plan:
To take them out of the creel, still struggling,
And run my hand across their scales,
Letting each one draw blood
With its dark fin. And if I've an oarsman's
Strength still, to drop them over the bow
And watch them swim under the keel,
Rejoicing as they ride the cold tide
Out to the great North Sea.

# MAIS OU SONT LES NEIGES D'ANTAN

*By a single line of verse in an almost forgotten language …*
*the name of Villon goes on living defiantly; our efforts,*
*as we seem to try to efface it, polish and make it shine*
*the more.*

William Carlos Williams


There is a poet who lives by one line,
throw everything else away:
the quatrain, catalogues, chant royal
— sustenant though they be —
he still leaves a legacy
of matchless rarity,
defying space and time.

*Prince: it's one hell of a line.*

# TRAIL MIX

In 1954 the most exciting city in the world
for me (and every other kid on my block)
was Battle Creek, Michigan.

I knew nothing of the battle fought there in 1825
near a juncture with the Kalamazoo River. How
two Native Americans used their "injun-uity"
to thwart the progress of two pioneers —
until they were "shot from guns."

I had yet to meet the new generation of marketing
men. Didn't know that I was being "segmented."
Couldn't see Dr. Frankenstein, armed with an MBA,
designing role-monsters for "pecuniary emulation."

I sent away for a nuclear submarine — a plastic
replica of the U.S. Nautilus. I'd fill it with baking
soda and bring it with me into the bathtub. It would
turn on its side, burp, sink to the porcelain bottom,
burp again and rise to the surface — propelled
by a stream of Arm & Hammer bubbles.

While the real U.S. Nautilus slid under the polar cap
I scraped together funds for the latest Kellogg's offers,
scotchtaping my quarters to the boxtops. And I raced

up the steps when I smelled the words *Battle Creek*
on one of those little brown packages in our mailbox.

Now, when I shop Safeway, I reach for the high-fiber
cereals and shield my oat bran from the pretty young
woman behind me, who lacks the x-ray vision needed
to see the scar on my belly. So I won't be tempted
to lie to her and say: "I eat *Froot Loops* myself.
The *Common Sense* is for my dead father."

I no longer get advice from Tom Mix or Sky King.
I no longer ache to be the first on my block
to get the silver whistle only dogs can hear.
At breakfast I read about daily percentages
of iron, zinc, niacin, vitamins A through D —
and weep, because, damn it, it's too late.

I am what I ate.

# SCARING VEGETARIANS

*a prayer to be said before dinner*

Stanislavski help me to help vegetarians feel
the pain of a single stringbean torn from its mother vine;
the anguish of broccoli brought to a slow boil;
the cruelty of the yuppie term *al dente;*
the ordeal of the kidnapped artichoke — a strapping
farm girl from Salinas — gang-banged by psychotic
rapists who can't climax till they eat her virgin heart;
who do kinky things to her felt-green skin
with mayonnaise and butter; then tear it to shreds,
mirthfully, with Ted Bundy's toothy brand of manic love.

I want them to simmer with the succulents;
be creamed to kingdom come with Jersey corn;
sautéed, puréed with baby carrots;
mashed to yellow yuck with giant yams.

I pray to César Chavez that their consciences be bruised
when they pass those produce trucks on the freeway —
crates of overripe tomatoes rattling up I-5
to Safeway or Alpha Beta death camps:
jeweled seed dribbling off the executioner's knife,
forever reft of native furrows east of Fresno.

Soul of Gandhi grant them water, milk,
eggs, cheese, butter and humility that comes
from more than merely flirting with starvation ...
from knowing this survival game
is neither clean nor kind — enslavement at best
for trillions of joyless cows and sexless chickens.

Nor will I leave unchallenged their great white
hope, *tofu* — nor unleavened bread; nor floury pita;
nor flavored beverage to grace their "chaste" refection:
I'll cry: *What have you done to the wheat?*
*the soybeans? sugar cane? Think twice*
*before you drink your minted tea.*

As I sink my capped teeth tragically
into this hamburger dripping with blood —
I want *them* to feel as complicit as *we.*

# POW

I look him over and almost want to cry.
Yet another of their adolescent "soldiers."
Undernourished body, filthy, lice-ridden
hair — teeth a good pediatric dentist
would consider a challenge to restructure.
Age? Our interpreter says, "Thirteen."

I light a Marlboro, relax, inhale the fumes
and as my cigarette drifts towards him,
trailing ash and smoke,
suddenly he's terrified,
convinced that tortures older men described
at the hands of a former enemy are about to begin.
He tries to be a soldier, grits his teeth,
shuts his eyes — and when I rise to disabuse him
multiplies into roomfuls of helpless children
cowering before strenuous lights
that can streak across a desert sky in minutes ...
think their way over TV cable or miles of empty sand,
searching for something of value.

"It's okay," I assure him, as I stub
my butt in the tray, and lay my hand
on his shoulder, "That is not our way."

"You have been captured by Americans.
You will be treated as a prisoner of war
in accord with Geneva conventions.
After you've showered and been deloused
and answered a few dozen questions
we will give you medical attention …
treat those open sores …
monitor your blood and urine.

There will be therapy, Levi clothes,
mineral water, coca cola, videos,
freedom to worship Allah, Metallica or Christ,
and hi-tech food. Watch out. The plate is hot."

## FINDING THE HEN

*An English teacher returns to the classroom after a bout with cancer. He asks a pupil to use the word "brood" in a sentence.*

You use the word "brood"
in the modern way
to chastise a sulking sister.

*Brood.* I ask you what it means.
You answer with a child's casual faith
in the shifting language of today.

It's good to be here again
on this little shoal of time
(not yet exposed by a Fowler
or covered by the OED)
to be a teacher again and hint
at all that brood once meant
to Milton, Hopkins, Yeats ....

I get a blue-jay feather from the bio-box
so you can touch a quill and maybe see
that a word need not be a paltry thing.

To make a word live
I must show you a playground
where every child is singing

in a sandbox full of unanticipated
shapes — castles not yet imagined.

I must help you savour a sound
that with its thrilling "r"
sings us into a golden trance
of avian motherhood.

I want you to go beyond abstraction
and see Tippy, the black game hen,
shivering in the snow-encrusted coop —
feel her feathery presence
and know
that God needs all the fiber
love can provide
to keep his eggs from breaking.

I want you to *brood.*
I want you to see your sister *brooding.*
I want you to flex *vaengir, fethra, wings* —
and be renewed.

## PARTING MY HAIR AT FIFTY-TWO

It comes down to a choice, to a parting
between "gray" and "grey." There is
a real difference in the sounds. A slight
"ehhh" if you spell it the British way.
A tighter, dryer, less colourful phoneme
for dealing with that *King Lear* sky
or foggy bureaucrat from *Bleak House.*
But "gray" to catch the optimism
of the President's silk tie —
elongating the vowel
to broaden the comedy
as he explains
the ins & outs
of *sacrifice.*

The old "grey" goose, Barbara Frietchie's old
"gray" head — or vice versa. "Gray" if you
want to show signs of life or garner sympathy.
But "grey" to describe that beat-up Triumph
with the customized license-plate, TIME —
now veering toward us, parting oleander,
as it drifts across the James Lick Freeway.

I'm talking about the color of my hair — "gray"
or "grey." Just another question of style. Though
the stakes are somewhat higher than when choosing
between "Demon Red," say, and "Hallelujah Green."

## UNREFINED

I'm vulgar.
If I were wheat I'd be bulgar.

If I were a bird I'd be *Crow*.
If I were absurd I'd be Pozzo.

If I were a Norse God I'd be Loki.
If I were a dance, the hokey-pokey.

Slip *me* the keys to the kingdom
and I'll let the riffraff come —
the leper, the beggar, the poet and the bum.

If I were on the surface, I'd be scum.

If I could put on strings, I'd be a ukulele
and if Segovia came, I'd say, "Sorry —
only Arthur Godfrey can strum me."

Things gross in nature become me.

I am the chaff which the wind driveth away
I am the human laugh of the feral child at play.

I'm the only man at the brothel
who still goes upstairs with *Olga!*

Even my rhyme is half-assed.
I'm vulgar.

## SOUL FOOD

I met the old man again last night
sitting by the side of the road.
I see more and more of him now
since my father died.

He asked me for food again.
All I had were a few Smith Brothers cough drops —
the black ones with the star in the middle
and the two sinister rabbis on the box ...
the licorice tasting ones I never liked ...
the ones I used to hide behind the bed
when my mother turned on the vaporizer
and left me perspiring in the dark.

I gave him the cough drops.
It was no big deal.
Not what you'd call "a real test."
Not like my Ph.D. orals
or having my colon resectioned.

He accepted them fastidiously
with dark, bony fingers,
his eyes shining with nervous-breakdown energy.
*He had so much to impart to the chosen son!*
Then he made a fist —
and they were *his* cough drops, not mine.

Once again he shared no magic.
Once again he gave no advice.
Once again he did not leave me beans.

Some nights I wake with a cry,
certain I am out of the  running —
that I've lost everything for lack of a few choice words
or a liverwurst sandwich I forgot to put in my sack.
That the old man teaches 101.
That the castle keep is empty.
That the task I must perform
has yet to be imagined or assigned.
That I'm not simple enough for him yet.
That he cares only for youth.
That he waits around in rest rooms like Verlaine,
saving everything for an *énfant terrible*.

As I shake out the sheets each morning
I keep looking for a crumb
from the Gingerbread House,
some ashes from the tinderbox,
a slice of the white snake,
a tiny strand of Rapunzel's hair …

something I can bring back to the lab
and put under a microscope …
something I can carry with me
to show nonbelievers where I've been.

# NOTES

*Page 6:* François Villon, whom I discovered in my high school library when I was sixteen, is an abiding spiritual voice in *Counterpoint*. The allusion in stanza two is to his celebrated *Quatrain* (translated Galway Kinnell):

> *I am François, which is my cross*
> *Born in Paris near Pontoise*
> *From a fathom of rope my neck*
> *Will learn the weight of my ass.*

*Page 7:* "and feel the way St. Joseph felt." See Yeats' "A Stick of Incense:"

> *Whence did all that fury come?*
> *From empty tomb or virgin womb?*
> *Saint Joseph thought the world would melt*
> *But liked the way his finger smelt.*

*Page 12:* *Polygonia interrogationis,* popularly called "the Question Mark," is named for the punctuation suggested by the silver marking on its underwing. Closely related is *Polygonia comma.*

*Page 27:* "Rollfast" is not a Norse god (as someone at a reading once theorized) but a $28 bicycle much used by middle-class kids in the forties.

*Page 32:* The author wants to thank First Interstate Bank's Automated Teller for helping with this poem.

*Page 37:* Graduate students are advised not to spend too much time looking for these lines in Walton. I went to the *Compleat Angler* certain that I would find an appropriate epigraph for "The Earthworm Odyssey" — but when Walton failed to oblige me, I made these lines up for him. From all I know of Izaak he was a sweet tempered fellow who wouldn't hold a little collaboration against me. Besides, his copyright has long since run out, interest in his work has waned (even amongst fishermen), and those few seventeenth century scholars who might rise to his defense are unlikely to read this book. (And why should they? Their time is better spent on Milton and Donne.)

Page 39: "diggory-delvet." See Beatrix Potter, *Appley Dappley's Nursery Rhymes*:

> *Diggory diggory delvet!*
> *A little old man in black velvet;*
> *He digs and he delves —*
> *You can see for yourselves*
> *The mounds dug by Diggory Delvet.*

Page 45: *The Great Tradition* is the title of F. R. Leavis' influential re-evaluation of the English novel (1948).

Page 52: Psittacosis (also called Parrot Fever) is one of the few diseases communicable from bird to human.

Page 53: "Wild Card" is dedicated to Jack Nicholson and to the memory of another joker, Cesar Romero.

Page 60: "Turtles are *nothings*." One should never underestimate the Lieutenant's erudition. Here we find him paraphrasing Robert Lowell's "The Neoclassical Urn:"

> *… A turtle's nothing. No*
> *grace, no cerebration, less free will*
> *than the mosquito I must kill —*
> *nothings! Turtles!…*

"Don't be like Liddy, Sir." The Lieutenant is referring to Watergate conspirator (now actor and radio talk show host) G. Gordon Liddy, who once held his hand in the flame of a candle to demonstrate his *machismo* to a young lady. The "hard gemlike flame" is of course another allusion to Walter Pater, who appears to be on the Lieutenant's literary shit-list.

Page 65: "Gulp the dead-black wine." Villon again. The allusion is to the final lines of *Le Testament* (translated by Galway Kinnell):

> *He took a swig of dead-black wine*
> *As he made his way out of this world.*

*Page 71:* *The Second Water Poet Reviews His Poems* was rejected by a literary journal whose policy is to assign both a writer and a scholar to read each submission. The writer said, "I just plain enjoyed this one but do not entirely trust my own judgment." The scholar protested that the poem is "not a credible recreation of the mid-seventeenth century," noting that "perch are fresh water fish and would not swim to the North Sea" whereas "mullet," being "warm-ocean fish," had no business being in the Thames at all. Pointing to other "inaccuracies" and "anachronisms," the scholar noted that "it is not easy to recreate the voice of a bygone age" and advised the author to "pay more attention to the dialogues of Restoration drama" before presuming to make further incursions onto his private turf.

*Page 75:* This epigraph is from William Carlos Williams' introduction to *The Complete Works of François Villon*, translated by Anthony Bonner, 1960.

*Page 76:* "pecuniary emulation." One of a number of notable phrases (the most famous being "conspicuous consumption") introduced by Thorstein Veblen in his *The Theory of the Leisure Class*.

*Page 82:* "not yet exposed by a Fowler." H. W. Fowler, author of the invaluable *A Dictionary of Modern Usage*. On the deterioration of 'brood' he has this to say: "One may brood on or over something, but not *about* it." Also pertinent are his entries on "cast-iron idiom" and "slipshod extension."

*Page 83:* "vaengir, fethra." Old Norse and Old English for "wings."